TO INHABIT THE FELT WORLD melds the exquisite cl⟨ poetry and art, with the personally sentient view of creativity displayed in her vivid autobiography *DRAWING THE LINE,* to create a triptych that guides a reader through the evolution of the human spirit and its myriad vestments —birth, death, grief, love, friendship, awe, and ultimately a return to the mutually human necessities of art and literature. The sinews of Ms. Gardner's poetic form elevate our own perceptions, so that we too, may unabashedly *inhabit the felt world* and restore those moments, which deem us human and aesthetically free.
– Gary Worth Moody, author of *HAZARDS OF GRACE*

ֆ ֆ ֆ

Susan Gardner writes "with no other proof but memory."
She urges us

"take one breath,
exhale
then one more."

Susan takes us by the throat to Toronto Island, Montserrat, the New York Library, a hospital, into seemingly veiled poems that leave haunting images for us to reinterpret, to meditate upon. These are poems for the poet-breath within us. One reading, one long breath is not enough. Within Susan Gardner's writing is the deep breath we take at the end of the book that says, I have heard the roar of a poet responding to the love and pain in a private, felt world.
As a fellow poet, I am revived by this gathering of penetrating tenderness.
– James McGrath, author of *AT THE EDGELESSNESS OF LIGHT, DREAMING INVISIBLE VOICES* and *SPEAKING WITH MAGPIES*

ֆ ֆ ֆ

Susan Gardner's spare but urgent collection of poems, *TO INHABIT THE FELT WORLD*, is "the roar of alive"....

I don't believe I have ever read lines of such ferocity, honesty and pain....
TO INHABIT THE FELT WORLD is a remarkable collection by a remarkable poet/painter/photographer.
– Elizabeth Raby, poet, author of *INK ON SNOW*

TO INHABIT THE FELT WORLD

Susan Gardner

RED MOUNTAIN PRESS

ISBN 978-0-9855031-1-6
Printed in the United States of America
Image Ratio, Santa Fe, New Mexico

RED MOUNTAIN PRESS
Santa Fe, New Mexico
www.redmountainpress.us

For RDR

Contents

I

GARDEN BENCH

Narrowing path

    overrun with elephant ears, birds-of-paradise,
    pampas grass, plumed with decay.

    Tentacles avid relentlessly accelerate.
    Sumptuous excess silences slow wind.

    In canopy leaves reach for sky.

Alone here, unlonely,
immolant joy.

Between seasons, angled apart, the stone rests on gray schist legs.

Each dry winter, cemented
    in their shrunken rigid waterless bed
        desiccated stems flake to dust.
        Leaves of streamside trees
        wait for July rain to decompose.

Each rainy summer night it sinks another iota toward its ancestral home
        amidst the bedrock
        of the river's underground channel
        tipping imperceptibly
        aslant in the slippery loam.

The path a dirt track, no longer wide enough for two people to pass,
once planted, now wild

        below steep rock steps a derelict fountain,
        verdigris-bronze head on the wall
        calcified mouth unable to spout the rainy runoff.

There the bench waited for decades.

Broken sun glints through heavy foliage.

Awake
        I dream the afternoon.

Words fall through cascade of air.

Lines found in any order,
reordered,
folded away,

found again,
foundered in the torrent
found sheltered
this reader of stone in the rain.

ଓଃ   ଓଃ   ଓଃ

Along a wide path,
      white with florescent light,
      white with cold empty shining air,
      immaculate, pristine, precise,
      five people, a crowd covered in blue,
      walk steady and resolute.

Awake
      on the rolling platform
      I dream back this sheltered garden.

The tiny black mystery, size of a fingernail, sends its life out
      in threads, ready to take mine in suicidal excess.
      They, steadfast under blue lights, mean to murder
      this malignant monster.

Silence and noise, garden leaves,
insects and wind, muffled footsteps

A stone in the river, washed smooth
by twenty years' absence,
lies wet in the sunshine.

Gentle in its muddy bed,
heavy in my hand now, its body
contains the igneous history of the world.

A wader in this stream,
I step in the icy flow and fall
against its solid actuality.

Atlantic Flight

sky snow

scumbled over the landscape
undulates under blue clouds

       late sun
       rose-red
       lavender-lake

half the spectrum broken
over the roiled surface

defined by ivory-black ribbons
of frozen rivers

no bird dares the winter sky

this titanium cylinder
radiant in the stratosphere
flies high in the face of sense

STICKS AND STONES

Black ink on stone landscape

    violet *Duan* volcanic tuff, blue-black *She* slate,
    obsidian, soft, gray river rocks

    clinging smell of charred carbon powder and glue
    rumors of friction wearing at stick and stone

    formless ink, boundless, becomes

        poem, book, pine branch painting
        letter of good-bye
        stain on the table.

Trees' living, long white cambium filaments

        cut, simmered, slurried
        held afloat
        in the warm bath

spill from the mold
onto old pine cousins in the sun

felt into paper.

A branchlet, trimmed, sanded, silk-tied

to badger and fox hairs,
soaked in rabbit glue, dripped clean,
straightforward.

Hand circles inside black boundary

water reflects from black surface
ink blackens
marbles over inkstone

slowly, slowly readies itself for the brush.

The lake of blackness spreads over anthracite well of grinding stone.

Ink pulled into paper

  inadvertent turnings
  thickness varied by pressure applied
   onto each felted fiber
   bleeds at the edges.

Time lengthens

  Brush relinquishes its charge,
  sets free the ink it carries

to inhabit the felt world.

SECURITY

    the pendent lodestar
        beckoning siren
    perjured the moon
    in its wobbly orbit

        celestial aldermen
    stars traipse through
    compassed trajectory
    under arms of the milky way

Deep Water

sun-stunned dark water
touches curved blue atmosphere
ultramarine horizon invisible

skin darkens in fevered summer air
sweat a salty sheen
black curls halo over reddening ears
legs stiff at water's boundary

plunge in, drown in brilliant delight
weightless, jubilant
float besotted

I learn to swim

Trilogy for My Daughter

I   *Humming Room*

Humming room
tube twists of plastic carry
      false pink of new blood
      the lie of another promise.

Eyes open round to compass the midnight crisis.
Inch long black hairs comma the white sheet.
No blue milk taste on lips or tongue. No tears
fall on falling lashes.

Muscles starve for oxygen.
Fingers unfist, swell, open.

Skin peels back
      fiery flesh
      too fragile to contain.

Through roughened surface,
the bloody serum
seeps through blistered layers.

Breaths frail. Thread-thin muscles
do not lift the three-inch ribs.
Cries whimper to silence.

White box, blue dress —
     less than one square yard of cotton to keep
     the brown dirt at bay.

Rotted together now.
Dirt. Dress. Girl.

II   *Memory's Shape*

With no other proof but memory exists that moon blue eye.

Black curl creeps over the edge of an ear.
Smile commits nothing more — or less — than this moment.

Trust an untrustworthy future.

Quiet room
        dark table with fat legs

        box big enough
        to hold a family's picnic

                standing in sunshine
                screaming
                speechless.

Hearts beat strong. Lungs
breathe

air you will never need. Brothers
cannot remember

your disappeared face.

My beloved
we are silent.

III　　***Pyre***

for Marian, who was with us more than a century

struggle, resist, gasp
to leave, defy necessity
renitent, obdurate want of life

mouth forms an O, tastes air,
eyes close, see only his long-ago face
skin tight over bone, wrinkleless

radiant life-light pours out into air
illuminates the passage

pyre's smoke steams to blue

portion
      to clouds
      to rain
measure
      small air

wash shards and ash of bone together
sink in earth   feed trees

return
      quaking yellow

tremble
      on our still faces

HOME BOUND

straw of summer flowers
held immobile, upright in snow

dirt tracks a frozen river of mud
refreeze in ruts half a foot deep

blue berries weight juniper trees
lean fence posts pull wire
shadows across iced fields

white-whiskered crane alone
in morning stillness
long feathers amidst brittle stems
eyes sweep cloud-struck sky
one path home

SNOWY DAY

for Marc Talbert

over pale summits no reflection
only motionless pewter sky

last year's piñon branches burn
resin scent traces through cold

at the window first flakes
on already fat lilac buds

drink chamomile tea
don't work, read poetry

sleep in the snowy fog

MONTSERRAT REVISITED

November drizzle dismisses easy days
      sky fog belts rocky towers
      last tenacious yellow cleaves to sycamore

Wet cobbles cross the village
      past sienna-plastered walls
      to the arched churchly porch

High-window light falls on young faces
      wide eyes, open mouths release ordinary voices
      celestial in the stone space

Long aisles interrupted with chapels
      virgin heroines long departed
      kings, conquerors, redeemers

One new brilliant glass-doored space, punctuated with
          crossed hands, crossed feet,
          thorned corona
      to enter, hands push the wooden bar
      caress the carved history of Catalunya

Gentle-voiced crowd edges around the perimeter
      up sloped steps scooped out by each pilgrim's foot
      the black Madonna, centuries of candled
      smoke and love shine on her face

Long promenade, black iron choirs
of fat, thin, tall, short,
red, green, white pillars
flame with hope

      outside people are passing by
      one more door

Red walls, shining wood floor, bright lights,
a room full of things

      two long white glowing wedding dresses
      sequins, embroidery, gathered stitching
      cover silk petticoats and sheer linings

black sleeves touch white silk
      a very short suit of black wool
      young brother to accompany the bride?
      stranger?

brass hooks hold
      small shoes
      plastic flowers
      infant's yellow bib
      summery straw hat
            with silk flowers around the crown

      tiny girl's starched pink dress
      white rickrack pristine
            no dribbles from a meal of applesauce

past the corner more hooks
a shelf with
      baskets
      music box
      chest with dark red velvet lining

Round another corner
     more flowers
     toys, photographs
     crutches

     sorrows
     gratitude

     A sign says
          everything
               all the objects
          are left behind

     and may yet be reclaimed

II

DESIDERATA

Desperate want.

To wake you at dawn,

    hands aflame, tongue fervent,
    skin blood burnished

    slake morning thirst with your sweet sweat
    scrawl my desires on your skin
    write my name on your mind

I want you to look at me in the dark
see me here
reborn

Body hungers.

Lips still, tongue fat, ears cold,
I want to stay
a while longer

     evade the desolation of your absence
     evoke your ghost to stroke skin, caress breast,

     assuage scorched spirit

to hold and have without end
your face in my hands

A great eagle
keen talons outstretched

soars over.

PARTITA   A TRILOGY

I   *Coffee break*

they lean into the space between them
faces illuminated with interest
or pheromones
they leave their coffee to grow cold

he explains
       the phenomenological world
       materialist dialectics
       kama sutra

blind to the world
they take one breath,
exhale
then one more

deaf to all but one voice,

bellies, breasts, crotch, hair

focused

limerance absolute

immeasurable, preposterous, unquenchable appetite

ravenous for bone and skin

avid for muscle, fat, blood

finger pads on webbing of toes

hair against breast, tongue edging earlobe,

voice in the valley

notched between clavicles

the roar of alive

II   *Lust*

He just wants

dominion over money, mind, body, over piles of flesh
       ownership of toes, taste buds, hips
       ownership of thought, intention, ambition
       piles of stuff no one wants

She holds hurt in her bones

       in mind
       in dreams
       at the edge
       of fingernails

       scraping the soul.

Two, cancered with regret

shrunk into a teaspoon of sown salt.

III   *Weight*

Hard tumor of hurt

No need for absolution

    Unrequited
    untouched
    no amends

left with fingers

bent backward off open palms,
calloused with unanswered forgiveness

SLOW WIND WALLOW

June 2011
>   *Fire burning 200,000 acres of Arizona.*

June 2012
>   *289,000 acres of New Mexico burning.*
>   *Biologists, crossing the fire line, corral*
>   *electro-stunned Gila trout.*
>   *Fish to spend summer vacation in northern New Mexico.*

Burning.
Burning up.
Burning down.

Dark clouds pass
snag on rocky crags

rain smoke
into our forest, our town, our skin

smoky glare fills Sunday morning

smoky air too heavy to drift away
over summits

microbits of Arizona
in our eyes
in our lungs

with us
now and forever
until we also are

microbits

GALAXY

In West Virginia red stripes of afternoon
meet the evening over village novas.

Each point in new dark
shines strands of light one to another.

The last of winter afternoon
glitters on past summer fertility,

ignites geometry of frozen irrigation
circles inside square girdles.

Ponds, still now,
show the last motion of fall.

Towns, hamlets, farms, stars reborn each night

blue and green light
against the newly black sky
and blacker night.

Vivid orange-yellow beacons
brush bold against the winter ground

glow white with halogen
some sharp as pins
some a little blurred in the center.

Still a trace of red sky beyond the grounded world.

III

New York Public Library

A book connects us to one another through time and space.
We hold the author's ideas in our hand
unmediated by anything except our own curiosity.

I

The children's room

      five steps above the main floor

      open shelves for young patrons

      librarian's desk near the door

Read pictures, read poems

      hushed pages rustle

      dust motes lift through window's shifting light

      bindings skate across silk-smooth golden maple

      quiet clicks stamp dates on paper slips

Borrow armfuls of books

Five steps down, secreted from infant eyes,
forbidden treasure

Necessary whispers only. Perfect.

II

Marble beasts before limestone columns
allow passage
across hundreds of steps

 mimes mug for nickels
 anxious lovers suspended in anticipation of one face
 arms overflow with books unaligned

  readers ascend to their shared home
  scholars climb the white flights
  earnest heads bow with weight of words

III

Double-storied coffered domes over stacks
      asylum for earth's every thought
          city's every scholar,
          idler, pencil-pusher,
                venerable, solitary,
                prized, repudiated
          aged and child
          have a place at this table

sounds brush through silent space
          talk soft at the desk
          pencils scribble
          shoes cross marble floors
          index fingers slide under corners
                impatient to turn pages
          everything we touch is paper

thoughts from yesterday and millennia before
seined in paged nets

On heads bent over books
brass lamps shine gold

           consolation for the lonely
           comfort for the cold
           solace for the bereft

stay until the midnight closing hour

TRAFFICKING

At the light
clocks tick

Idling bodies shimmer through
glare, mob momentarily at rest

Flame-painted
remains rise in the heat

Antediluvian fossils
forgotten faces
undeciphered
volatile vapors
still

Now
the time
the indefinite sometime
has arrived

THAT DAY

Knock your elbow against the edge of the door,
the funny bone sends a thrill of shock
right to your brain.

On this hot morning
our eyes knock.

In that instant
                every bone funny
                every muscle laughing
                every hair breathless.

In the aftershock keep touching
that electric pain
lean against the doorframe
until our hearts can move again.

SPRING SUITE

Clement

this fine rainy day
clouds scud in wind
chase isobars of cold across
iced spring jet stream

Early Harvest

tomato blossoms explode
in yellow dismay

silky flames flare
in icy rain

Frozen Bloom

overnight
virgin pinks shrivel to brown
moonlit frost

fertility lost
to cold April

Toronto Island Early Morning

clouds rest on grassy ground

no shadows cast
no darkness mars the light
no glint amends silent morning

Audacious Claimant

lake pretender aspires to be ocean
wind brings storm and lake-sea is its leader
waves just wannabes

beach trees bow well over
backs of their leaves greet
slanting stinging not yet
wet air

Cold River

the river runs cold now
flavored with last year's ice

around water-soft rocks
it pools clean and frigid
rushes to oceanic oblivion

WAITING: FALL

For Love of Red

       red silk wet on pine needles
       maple and sumac glimmer red against the road
       neither is red as the red wool blanket
       in my blue room

Evensong

       coyote families sing the dusk
            sun flares redden mountains
          sky blue as lapis lazuli
       until moonless black uncovers stars

Cold

blue scraps of sky
crack out of clouds

dull winter ground
rigid brown

soon
snow we've longed for

Storm

clouds bank black against less black mountains
flying snow crosses dusky sun
fractured into winter rainbow

Red Twig

morning fog lifts its wet weight
red twig shines
in remembrance

clouds in a prism of urgency
rush to the sea

an insect pauses
lost in last summer's litter

Sidereal

night draws each body
over moonless horizon

Jupiter rises
stars overwhelmed
orbit toward dawn

Fog

shapeless quiet slides over the roof
colors hide

in deepening dusk
rain channels bark

fog drips on a forest mouse
somewhere near   a song

WHITEOUT: TWENTY PERFECT MINUTES

All night we lie

          in the comfort of our white bed

under our white comforter

while snow slides over the mountain

          and lies down over everything

In the morning feeble sun

          glimmers down

          until the cloud-blanket evaporates

in great sheets of silence

Not one eighth of a millimeter
    space enough
        unbounded
          extravagant
          uncontested
          unconditional

    for prairies of quarks and muons
    to find themselves locked in atomic attachment

Not one eighth of a millimeter
    from you, I am
        profligate
         spendthrift
          improvident

    imprudent enough to fill galactic silences
    shriek strings
    across the frozen black topography

    to grace the electrons of our nucleus

Not a molecule struck by lightning
     not one breath inhaled
     then released into planetary atmosphere
     not the thickness of thread is
between us

Only the length of that thread
     twisting
       stretching
         lengthening

to the necessary

infinity

Nothing between us
but this hour

PHYSICS OF THE IRIS

Iris, courier of the gods, uses her rainbow to carry
messages between earth and heaven.

the body of one

      raging with joy

      against the surface of the other

in a cloud, as far apart

      as infrared and ultraviolet

      as hydrogen and oxygen

the spectrum broken open

      electric songs

      resounding

delirium of molecules let loose

      critical mass achieved

Iris flying home with old news

Acknowledgements

I thank Elizabeth Raby for her discerning questions and friendship, Gary Worth Moody for insightful reading, literary courage, and more than one push in the right direction, and Moriah Williams for care and thoughtfulness in editing.

One more time, RD has supported and encouraged work that once would have been unimaginable and now is inevitable.

Susan Gardner
Santa Fe, 2013

To Inhabit the Felt World is set in Palatino,
a 20th century font designed by Hermann Zapf
based on the humanist type fonts of the Italian Renaissance
and named for the 16th century Italian master of calligraphy
Giambattista Palatino.